Wrestling
Greats

BOBO
BRAZIL

by Ross Davies

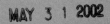
The Rosen Publishing Group, Inc.

Published in 2001 by the Rosen Publishing Group, Inc.
29 East 21st Street, New York, NY 10010

Copyright © 2001 by The Rosen Publishing Group, Inc.

First Edition

Library of Congress Cataloging-in-Publication Data

Davies, Ross.
Bobo Brazil / by Ross Davies.— 1st ed.
p. cm.— (Wrestling greats)
Includes bibliographical references (p.) and index.
ISBN 0-8239-3431-4 (lib. bdg.)
1. Brazil, Bobo—Juvenile literature. 2. Wrestlers—
United States—Biography—Juvenile literature. [1. Brazil,
Bobo. 2. Wrestlers. 3. African Americans—Biography.] I.
Title. II. Series: Davies, Ross. Wrestling greats.
GV1196.B6 D38 2001
796.812'092—dc21

00-012713

Manufactured in the United States of America

Contents

Bobo Brazil was, and is, a true wrestling legend and pioneer.

The Pioneer

The day will be remembered forever, not only in the history of Major League Baseball, but also in the history of the United States. On April 15, 1947, the Brooklyn Dodgers ran onto the field for their first game of the season at Ebbets Field in Brooklyn. That day, all eyes in the stadium were on one man—Jack "Jackie" Roosevelt Robinson—who with the first pitch of the game became the first African American to play in the major leagues.

That season, four other African American men followed Robinson into the major leagues: Larry Doby, Henry Thompson, Willard Brown, and Dan Bankhead. Robinson, however, is the one who has gone down in history as the man who broke baseball's color barrier. American sports haven't been the same since.

"I know that I am a black man in a white world," Robinson said. "I know that I never had it made."

Robinson was a pioneer because he was the first. He was a hero because he endured the threats and taunts of fans and teammates and went on to a Hall of Fame career. Today, the number 42 he wore has

On April 15, 1947, Brooklyn Dodger Jackie Robinson broke the color barrier in Major League Baseball.

been retired by every team in Major League Baseball.

The situation wasn't quite the same for Bobo Brazil. No heads turned when Brazil wrestled his first match because by the time Brazil made his professional wrestling debut in 1950, ring sports had long been open to African Americans. In 1938, boxer Joe Louis had become an American hero when he defeated German Max Schmeling for the heavyweight championship.

But before Bobo Brazil, there was no such thing as a black man holding a major United States heavyweight title. Said Burrhead Jones, who teamed with Brazil in the 1960s, "Bobo Brazil was to wrestling what Jackie Robinson was to baseball."

In 1994, the World Wrestling Federation bestowed upon Bobo its highest honor by inducting him into the Hall of Fame. In 1961, wrestling journalist Walter Ford wrote, "The most noticeable thing about Bobo Brazil is his amazing popularity with fans of all colors, shapes, sizes, and creeds. In an era where racial prejudice is still rampant in many fields and areas, it is refreshing to see this big, dusky hero taken to the hearts of so many people. It seems that Bobo is so completely heroic that he overcomes all potential resistance before it ever begins."

At the time Bobo started wrestling in the 1950s, there were hardly any African American professional wrestlers. After all, what was the point? They didn't get the same opportunities as white wrestlers. They weren't given title matches. They could only wrestle other African Americans. Although professional wrestling did not have a policy prohibiting African Americans from wrestling, the attitudes of the time made it difficult for a black man to make a living in the ring.

"He was sort of an idol because there were so few black wrestlers around back then," the Reverend Donald Adkins told the *Herald-Palladium* newspaper of Benton Harbor, Michigan. "Everybody loved him, especially the kids."

It was also unusual for an African American wrestler to be popular with all fans, no matter what their heritage or racial background. The man the fans loved was big. He stood 6'4" and weighed 280 pounds. He dressed stylishly, wrestled flamboyantly, walked with a purpose, and spent virtually his entire career as a favorite of wrestling fans. He had a deep, distinguished voice and a deep chuckle. He laughed long and hard, and his long, slick-backed hair was always immaculately combed. He was a television star who rarely went against the rulebook. He won nine National Wrestling Alliance United States heavyweight championships. Until Bobo came along, that belt had never been won by an African American.

"Bobo Brazil was the most famous black wrestler of his day," wrote Killer

Kowalski in the magazine *Wrestling Then & Now.* "His groundwork made it possible for other black wrestlers to follow in his steps."

Bobo helped change the life of every African American wrestler who came after him. In 1992, Ron Simmons became the first African American to win the World Championship Wrestling world heavyweight title. Today, The Rock—who is part black, part Samoan—is one of the most famous and popular wrestlers in the world.

But Bobo Brazil wouldn't say that they owe him anything. He was just doing what he loved to do.

Growing Up Poor

The man who came to be known as Bobo Brazil was born Houston Harris in 1924 in Little Rock, Arkansas. He was the third of six children—three boys, three girls. The Harris family never had much money. They moved from Arkansas to East St. Louis, Illinois, and then to Benton Harbor, Michigan, where Houston spent most of his childhood. Houston's father died when he was seven. His mother, Ruby, and his grandfather, Ivy Jones, raised Houston and his siblings.

Money didn't come easily to the Harris family. Grandpa Ivy had a farm just outside of town, but the farm didn't produce enough income to support a family of eight. Because of this, Houston's days were long and difficult. He went to school during the day and when he got out of school, he went to work. During the summer, he and his brothers picked fruit at various orchards around Benton Harbor— a city that was well known for its apples, peaches, and cherries.

"We'd go out early every morning and work until late afternoon," Bobo said in a 1964 magazine interview. "The fruit trees were pretty high. We climbed stepladders for the picking. Going up those ladders, I had the feeling I was an old-time sailor climbing the masts. A fall from that height could have been rough."

The workers placed the fruit they picked into big containers called lugs. They received fifty cents for each lug they filled. Houston's strength and motivation led him to filling three or four lugs a day. In the 1930s, two dollars a day was a lot of money for a poor family.

"The $1.50 or $2.00 I took home seemed like a fortune to me," Bobo said. "The money was hard to come by. Funny thing, we never knew we were poor. Always had a nice clean bed to sleep in. Always had good, solid food on the table. No extras, but all the essentials were there."

The summers were happy times for Houston. He was big for his age and extremely athletic. He got his kicks from playing baseball. No matter how tired he was after a long day's work in the orchards, he'd run home, grab a bite to eat, then run back outside to meet his friends on the baseball field. They'd play until it was dark and they could no longer see the ball.

While growing up, Houston never gave a thought to professional wrestling. He didn't wrestle in high school— instead, he was a teenage base- ball star. Houston was an outfielder and

"The $1.50 or $2.00 I took home seemed like a fortune to me."

-Bobo Brazil, on growing up

a power hitter who could drive the ball farther than most adults. When he was seventeen years old, his team won the sandlot championship. The team had Houston to thank for the win.

This was the early 1940s and Jackie Robinson was six years away from playing in the major leagues. If an African American was good enough to play professional baseball, he did so in the Negro Leagues, or for one of the many independent teams that toured the United States. One of those independent teams was located in Michigan. The House of David team was good enough to beat most of the other independent teams around the country. A week after Houston's team won the sandlot

As depicted in the 1952 movie, *Alexander, the Big Leaguer,* members of the House of David baseball team, which Houston Harris would join in the early forties, did not shave for religious reasons.

championship, a representative from the House of David approached him.

"We want you to play for us," the man told him. "You'll play first base and you'll be in the starting lineup right away."

Houston hesitated for a few minutes. The House of David was a religious sect that believed it was against God's will to shave. All of the team members had very long beards. Houston didn't even have a day's growth.

"He told me I wouldn't have to grow a beard," Bobo recalled. That's how badly the team wanted him.

Houston played in Cleveland, Memphis, and Michigan during his first week on the House of David team. The crowds were huge and Houston had a great time. After the first week, the man who ran the team walked up to Houston and handed him a check for $300. For a teenager who had been making two dollars a day filling fruit containers, that was a huge amount of money.

"I thanked him a dozen times and told him I would have played a month for that," Bobo recalled.

Houston's later paychecks wouldn't be for quite as much money, but they were enough that he could help out his family, put food on the table, and still have plenty of spending money left over.

Houston was having the time of his life. He had exceeded his wildest dreams.

3 The Birth of the Coco Butt

One day in 1950, wrestler Joe Savoldi had an afternoon free before his match that night in Minneapolis, Minnesota. Savoldi, a former star football player for legendary coach Knute Rockne at the University of Notre Dame, was a big baseball fan. He decided to go out and watch the Minneapolis Millers baseball team play. One player in particular caught his eye.

"He hit like Babe Ruth, fielded like Jackie Robinson, and did everything with a raw, animal-like power that, properly controlled, would make a great star of him," Savoldi recalled in a 1961 interview with *Wrestling Review* magazine. "But I saw something else in him. I saw a tremendous physique going to waste. Ball players have to be good athletes, sure, but sometimes you find one who could do something else even better, if he only tried."

The player was Houston Harris, who by 1950 had moved from the House of David team to the Millers. Houston continued to impress Savoldi as he helped his team win the game. After the game, Savoldi approached him in the locker room.

"Ever think about being a wrestler?" Savoldi asked Houston.

"No," Houston replied. "And I don't intend to think about it, either. Jackie Robinson went up to the big time a long time ago and I intend to be next."

Savoldi, a stubborn man, wouldn't take no for an answer.

"You're wasting your time," Savoldi insisted. "By wrestling for a living, you can make twenty times what you're making now, and get a lot less dirty."

"I wouldn't wrestle for a living," Houston said, "even if I had to go on relief."

Savoldi invited Houston to come to the wrestling card that night to watch him wrestle. Houston said he'd be there. After all, he didn't have anything better to do. After the matches, Savoldi asked

Joe Savoldi convinced Houston Harris to consider professional wrestling as a career.

Houston what he thought. Houston just shrugged his shoulders. But Savoldi saw a gleam in the young man's eyes.

"I could have let him slip through my fingers right there, but no, I know talent when I see it, and besides, there's as much of a challenge in finding a new star as there is in being one," Savoldi later said.

Shortly afterward, Houston was invited by Savoldi to attend another card at the Benton Harbor Naval Armory. During the card, a wrestler issued a challenge to anyone in the audience who thought he could keep up with him in the ring. The prize was fifty dollars. Savoldi picked Houston out of the audience. Houston didn't last long enough in the ring to win the money, but he impressed Savoldi, who was surer than ever that the ballplayer had what it took to become a wrestler. After the card, Savoldi finally convinced Houston to give wrestling a try.

Once Savoldi started working with Houston in the gym, he saw that his hunch that the young athlete would make a good wrestler was correct. As good as he was at baseball, Houston was even better at professional wrestling.

"In the very beginning, he wanted to go back to playing ball," Savoldi said of the young Houston.

In wrestling training sessions, athletes go all out for hours under strenuous conditions. This was a lot tougher than baseball training sessions, where players spend a lot of time standing around the batting cage or waiting to have a ball hit to them.

Two important things happened during Houston's training sessions with Savoldi. Houston changed his name to Bobo Brazil, and Savoldi helped Bobo create his most famous move, the Coco Butt.

"Joe [Savoldi] felt that every part of your body should be in shape," Bobo said in a 1963 interview. "So Joe brought a piece of plywood with him one day to the gym and had me butting my head against it. Talk about headaches. I really had them the first couple of months. Finally, it got to the point where I began to crack the wood and only then did Joe feel that my head was hard enough.

"I didn't know what Joe had in mind," Bobo continued. "I thought he was toughening up my head for any hard falls I might take in the ring. But he made me put that training to a better use—I would pull my opponent toward me, hold the back of his head, and bump him on the forehead with my forehead."

Bobo not only learned how to use his head, but he learned how to put his athleticism to good use, too. Although Bobo was big enough to win by punching, kicking, and overpowering his opponents, Savoldi wanted Bobo to know how to wrestle.

"We developed the abdominal stretch, where I wrap my left leg around my opponent's right leg, around and behind and then take my left arm and go under his right arm," Bobo said. "It's a submission hold and not too many have broken it."

After five months of intense training, Savoldi sent Bobo to Toronto, Canada, to wrestle in his first official match. Bobo had never been so nervous in his life. He had stood in batting boxes staring down pitchers throwing ninety mile per hour fastballs, but that was nothing like the pressure he faced that night at Maple Leaf Gardens.

"I quit. I'll stick to baseball!"

-Bobo Brazil

There were 14,000 fans in the building. Bobo couldn't relax. He paced around the locker room, waiting for his match to start. Savoldi, his mentor, wasn't there to help him this time. Bobo would have to get by on his own.

That night, Bobo beat Hans Hermann, a wrestler who has long since been forgotten. After the match, Bobo walked out of the ring battered and exhausted. His bones ached and when he got up the next day, he could barely move. He felt horrible. He missed baseball. He picked up the phone and called Savoldi.

"I quit!" Bobo told him. "I'll stick to baseball."

As usual, Savoldi wouldn't take no for an answer. He booked Bobo for matches that week in other Canadian cities—Hamilton, London, and Kingston. Bobo got back in the ring and kept working. He kept trying, and kept taking his lumps. And he kept winning matches.

"It was never a snap," Bobo said. "It was always tough, even against second-raters. A man who's tough enough to wrestle for a living is no cinch for anybody to beat. You got to work to win and you're bound to get hurt somewhere along the line. You just have to forget about the pain and just go on wrestling. After a few years of it, you're a wrestler. That's when you start enjoying it."

When that first week ended, Savoldi sent Bobo a check for $2,200—a lot more than the $300 he had received for his first week of baseball, and a ton more than the two dollars a day he had once made picking fruit.

"I was staggered, as well as delighted," Bobo recalled. "How could I keep playing ball when there was this sort of money in wrestling?"

The answer: He couldn't. Bobo put aside his dream of following Jackie Robinson into the major leagues. After all, he had already arrived in the major leagues ... of professional wrestling.

4 A Midwestern Her

During his first year as a professional wrestler, times weren't always so great for Bobo. Some nights, he would drive 200 miles from Benton Harbor to Detroit just to get paid three dollars for a match. He struggled to get noticed, partly because his wrestling personality was a rulebreaker—a villain, or bad guy. Being a bad guy didn't fit his personality. In Benton Harbor, the fans knew their hometown wrestler wasn't a bad guy at all.

Promoter Joe Mackowitz was so impressed by Bobo's reputation that he placed Bobo in the main event in the wrestler's first match in the western United States.

"I started out as a bad guy, but the fans at the old armory wouldn't buy me as a bad guy," Bobo said later on in his career. "Then I became the good guy and things really changed for me."

After the ever-popular Bobo became a big drawing card, he made his first tour of the western United States. His first stop was in San Francisco. Wrestling promoter

Joe Mackowitz told Bobo, "I've heard big things about you." In his first match, Bobo was placed in the main event against Hombre Montana at the Cow Palace. Although he had been wrestling for over a year, Bobo was nervous. Nerves and all, Bobo soon settled down and beat Montana in twenty minutes.

"It was a big win for me," Bobo told *Wrestling World* magazine. "I felt confident. It was something I really needed. Between 'Frisco and Los Angeles, I managed to hold my own in bouts against Ray Stevens, Mike Sharpe, and others."

During his first two years, Bobo had been accompanied on the road by trainer Jimmy Mitchell. Now that he finally felt comfortable in the ring, Bobo told Mitchell to go home. Bobo formed an outstanding tag team with Leo Nomellini. California wrestling fans were thrilled by their ring exploits. Bobo and Nomellini had spectacular bouts against such teams as Mike and Ben Sharpe, and Lord Blears and Gene Kiniski, among others.

Having conquered the West Coast, Bobo decided that it was time to see another part of the world. Pedro Martinez, a promoter in Buffalo, had heard about Bobo and sent him a telegram, inviting him to come to western New York. Bobo willingly accepted the invitation and quickly became one of the biggest draws Martinez ever had.

Bobo was dominant in the ring. In his first four bouts, he beat Wild Bill Austin in thirteen seconds; Sky Hi Lee in twenty-nine seconds; felled Jim Bernard with a series of dropkicks in twenty-three seconds; then set a Buffalo record when he pinned Harry Lewis in only nine seconds. Bobo had won his first four matches in his new surroundings in a combined seventy-four seconds.

Bobo's career was taking off. He had great matches against superstar Gene Kiniski. He teamed with Yukon Eric, Whipper Billy Watson, Billy Lyons, and Ilio Di Paolo—some of the top

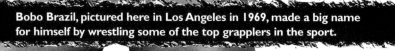

Bobo Brazil, pictured here in Los Angeles in 1969, made a big name for himself by wrestling some of the top grapplers in the sport.

wrestling stars of the 1950s. Baseball was a distant memory.

"Wrestling has been good to me and I doubt whether I could have made the grade as a major league baseball player," Bobo said in a magazine interview. "The friends I have made and the purses I receive from my matches have been a happy medium of existence for me. I do not know of any other sport or business that could have given me the same returns or the same rosy outlook on life."

Bobo also had outstanding matches against Killer Kowalski and Gorgeous George, who at the time was the most famous TV wrestler in the world. Bobo wrestled National Wrestling Alliance

Gorgeous George gets help preparing to make a grand entrance to the ring.

World Champion Lou Thesz in front of 15,000 fans. Back then, it was almost unheard of for a black wrestler to get a world title shot. Bobo wrestled gallantly, but lost the best two-of-three falls match in three falls. The match was the highlight of his life. He had learned a lot just from wrestling the legendary Thesz.

"I was so nervous," Bobo told newspaper reporters after the match. "To get in the ring with Lou Thesz, who's held the world title for so long, was a great thrill. I just hope that next time I'll be able to beat him."

In 1958, Bobo teamed with Whipper Watson to beat Reggie Lisowski and Stan Lisowski for the Canadian Open tag team title.

Life outside the ring was also going well for Bobo—he got married. Bobo and his wife, Leonora, had their first of six children, and he opened a bar in St. Louis, Illinois, called the Dew Drop Inn. When Bobo was in town, he would get behind the bar and serve customers. When he went out on the road, his brother managed the bar for him. Although Bobo was lonely on his long trips, Leonora would often travel hundreds of miles to watch her husband wrestle.

Bobo was becoming a major star in the Midwest. He packed the Benton Harbor Naval Armory during the 1950s and early 1960s for matches against the biggest names in pro wrestling—Dick the Bruiser, Killer Kowalski, Brute Benard, The Sheik,

Bobo puts an armlock on Skull Murphy, who he beat in eight minutes and two seconds at Madison Square Garden in June, 1962.

Gorgeous George, Buddy Rogers, Magnificent Muraco, Johnny Valentine, Haystacks Calhoun, Bruno Sammartino, and others. Although he wrestled in some of the most famous arenas in the United States and in front of crowds of over 10,000 people, the tiny Naval Armory was Bobo's favorite building. It was home, and he was the favorite of the hometown fans. Bobo was the local boy who made good.

"He was tough," the Reverend Donald Adkins informed the Benton Harbor *Herald-Palladium*. "He was a clean wrestler and was always respected by people."

There were bad times, too. In 1954, Bobo missed a drop kick against Great

Bolo and cracked a shoulder bone. Bobo had to stop wrestling for six months. However, during that time, he found a new love—fishing.

Bobo wowed fans with his sequined jackets and matching boots and tights. Bobo had his initials sewn onto the sides of his wrestling boots. He loved visiting children—his "little champs"—in hospitals.

And he was their big hero.

Go East, Young Man 5

When the 1960s began, African Americans were still a bit of a rarity in professional wrestling. Bobo, who by that time was being billed by promoters as "The Negro World Heavyweight Champion," wasn't interested in being different. He wanted to be treated the same as everyone else. The 1960s were the dawn of the black civil rights movement in the United States, and Bobo would play a small, but significant, role in the cause.

In the state of Indiana, until 1960, whites wrestled whites and blacks wrestled blacks. On December 6 of that year, a standing room only crowd of 3,200 wildly screaming fans packed the Indianapolis Armory for what would be an historic night. They were there to see a black wrestler fight a white opponent for the first time in the history of the state. Bobo's opponent was Hans Hermann, whom he had faced many times. Bobo was magnificent. He dominated the match from the opening bell and beat Hermann within a matter of seconds.

"I was awfully excited and awfully nervous," Bobo said after the match. "Nervous because I was accomplishing a

Bobo moves to subdue an opponent in a 1962 match at Madison Square Garden.

first in athletics for my race in Indiana, and also because I wanted to prove to the fans who were screaming and yelling their best wishes to me at ringside that I was worthy of their support. I was in the ring this night because I lived up to the standards of true American sportsmanship, and according to the concept that all humans are created equal."

Bobo was well on his way to becoming a superstar. In late 1960, Bobo started his first major feud—against Dick the Bruiser. Bruiser was the NWA United States heavyweight champion. The United States title was defended in Illinois, Michigan, Ohio, Indiana, and sometimes in western Ontario. The Brazil vs. Bruiser matches headlined numerous cards and attracted many sellout crowds to Cobo Hall in Detroit. Dick the Bruiser was the rule-breaker and Bobo was the fans' favorite. In two matches, the Bruiser almost crippled Brazil and won on what were widely regarded as flagrant rule violations.

Angered by Dick the Bruiser's actions, Brazil demanded and received a

Bobo finally overcomes Dick the Bruiser, one of his greatest rivals, for the NWA U.S. heavyweight championship in 1961.

rematch at the IMA Auditorium in Flint, Michigan. The match was designated as best-of-three falls with a ninety-minute time limit. Bobo vowed he would need no more than thirty minutes to destroy the Bruiser, and he predicted that the Bruiser would leave the ring on a stretcher.

"He doesn't have a chance against me tonight," Bobo vowed to reporters.

But Dick the Bruiser won the match in three falls. Heartbroken, Bobo refused to give up. His resiliency was rewarded and on January 28, 1961, in Detroit, Bobo pinned Dick the Bruiser for his first NWA U.S. heavyweight title. Bobo was the first African American to win the belt.

"This is like living a dream for me," Bobo said after the match. "I never had any doubt that I would beat him, but now that I really have beaten him and have this belt wrapped around my waist, I feel like I never want to let it go."

Unfortunately, Bobo's first title reign didn't last long. He lost the belt to Dick the Bruiser on February 28, 1961, in Detroit. But Bobo had gotten a taste of what it was like to be a champion. He wasn't the "black" NWA U.S. heavyweight champion; he was the only NWA U.S. heavyweight champion.

Buoyed by his success and acceptance from all of his fans, Bobo made an important phone call in the spring of 1962. At the time, a wrestler hadn't really made it big until he wrestled

Bobo Brazil puts a punishing move on Dick the Bruiser in a 1957 match in Chicago.

Bobo Brazil gets the upper hand against Gorilla Monsoon at New York's Madison Square Garden on December 16, 1963. The match was a draw.

in important matches in Washington, D.C. and in Madison Square Garden in New York. The most important man in East Coast wrestling was Vince McMahon Sr. (the father of current World Wrestling Federation owner Vince McMahon).

"Vince," Bobo said over the phone, "do you have any spots for me around Washington and New York?"

"We always have spots for a good man, Bobo," McMahon replied.

"We always have spots for a good man, Bobo."

-Vince McMahon Sr.

McMahon had heard about Bobo and had a lot of respect for him. He also knew that just because a man was a star in Los Angeles and Des

Moines didn't necessarily mean that he'd be a hit in Chicago and Memphis, or in New York. McMahon decided to give Bobo a try at some small clubs. If things worked out, Bobo would compete at the wrestling mecca known as Madison Square Garden.

Bobo didn't disappoint. One night in Alexandria, Virginia, after Bobo had won a tryout match, ecstatic fans transported him from the ring on their shoulders. As popular as he had been in the Midwest, Bobo was even more popular on the East Coast. McMahon was impressed and immediately booked Bobo to wrestle at Madison Square Garden. The New York fans loved him, too.

"I cannot recall any wrestler coming into my territory who was accepted so quickly and enthusiastically as Bobo," McMahon said. "So far as I am concerned, he can stay just as long as he wants to. And I promise to give him the opportunity to wrestle for the championship. I personally believe that he has an excellent chance to beat Buddy Rogers sometime within the next twelve months."

Buddy Rogers was the NWA world heavyweight champion. At the time, the NWA world title was the most important heavyweight championship in North America, meaning that Bobo Brazil was a pro wrestling superstar.

The Night Bobo
Wrestled Kiniski

6

Early in his life, Bobo Brazil had dreamed of becoming a major league baseball player. It was a dream that would never became a reality. But Bobo's next dream—becoming a successful professional wrestler—was different. This was a dream he would achieve, along with becoming a major star in the wrestling cities of the world.

One dream, however, remained elusive for Bobo. He wanted to win the NWA world title, but he couldn't seem to pin down champion Buddy Rogers for a match. Bobo waited patiently and never complained. He focused his efforts on moving up the ladder of title contention by beating other challengers. Finally, Bobo earned his shot against Rogers. But on the night of the scheduled match against Rogers at Madison Square Garden, the champion withdrew because of a slight concussion.

"I thought tonight would be it," Bobo told *Wrestling World* magazine. "I really was pointing toward this one. I was ready physically and psychologically. But that's the breaks. If Rogers isn't at his best physically, then I wouldn't want to face him with any so-called advantage. I want a good, clean shot at the title."

Unfortunately, it wasn't meant to be—at least not a championship match against Rogers.

On the night of April 25, 1963, Bobo won and lost the United States heavyweight championship at Maple Leaf Gardens in Toronto. Bobo's opponent was the great Johnny Valentine, one of the most ruthless rulebreakers of the time. When Bobo pinned Valentine, it seemed as though he had won the title. However, after being pinned, Valentine flopped one foot over the bottom strand of the ropes; according to wrestling rules, the entire bodies of both men must be completely in the ring at the time a pin is made. The referee saw Valentine's foot hanging over the ropes, but didn't realize that Valentine had put it there after the pin. Bobo's pin was ruled illegal. By that time, Bobo had already started celebrating his victory. Before the referee could inform Bobo that the match had been restarted, Valentine rushed up behind him and delivered his "brain crusher"—thrusting his elbow into Bobo's spine. Bobo fell to the mat and Valentine covered him for the pin.

In 1963, a group of Northeast promoters, led by Vince McMahon Sr., broke away from the NWA to form the World Wide Wrestling Federation—known today as the WWF. Bruno Sammartino won the WWF World heavyweight title from Buddy Rogers, which was both good and bad news for Bobo. It was good because Bobo hated Rogers and didn't want him to be the champion. But it was bad because both Bobo and Sammartino were favorites of the fans. In those days, in a world title match, promoters never signed one fan favorite to wrestle another. Bobo, however, was never lacking for opponents. In November 1963, he wrestled sadistic villain Fritz Von Erich in Indianapolis, Indiana. Von Erich—famous for his Iron Claw finishing maneuver—dug his steel-like fingers into Bobo's exposed stomach. To Bobo, it felt as if Von Erich was tearing big chucks of flesh out of him.

"To this day, I still don't know how I managed to walk out of that ring alive," Bobo told *Inside Wrestling* magazine years later. "But my stomach has never been the same since then."

Then Von Erich clamped his claw on Bobo's face.

"I was horrified by the thought that he was going to rip the skin right off my face," Bobo said.

Bobo survived that terrifying night in Indiana, but he couldn't overcome the whims of promoters. Sammartino would hold onto the WWWF world title for the next eight years and Bobo would never get his much-yearned-for title shot. Frustrated, Bobo turned his attention to one of the most hated wrestlers in the sport's history— The Sheik. Starting in 1963, Bobo and The Sheik feuded in wrestling matches around the world for the next decade. In August 1967, Bobo beat The Sheik for his second NWA United States title. Two months later, Bobo lost the belt to The Sheik.

On June 25, 1968 in Nagoya, Japan, Bobo did what few other wrestlers had ever done—he pinned Giant Baba, the seven-foot-tall Japanese wrestling superstar. After news of the victory spread, Japanese fans turned out in droves to watch Bobo. He won Japan's international heavyweight title and held it for only two days before losing it to Baba in Tokyo. Despite the loss, Bobo's earlier victory had made him a huge star in Japan.

Bobo still harbored world championship dreams, so he turned his attention to the NWA world title that had been held by Gene Kiniski since 1966. Kiniski was small, fast, and very talented. Bobo was granted a match against Kiniski.

At the time, Bobo vs. Kiniski was one of the biggest sports events in the history of Los Angeles. The match was to be held on December 18, 1968. But before the day arrived, there were many television interviews and press luncheons to attend. During a pre-bout television interview, tensions flared and Kiniski and Bob engaged in a fist fight.

The match lived up to all of the hype. Kiniski, who was rarely afraid, was terrified. He had been suffering from severe headaches and was concerned about getting Coco-Butted by Bobo. When the bell rang, Bobo used dropkicks and shooting scissorholds aimed at Kiniski's head. Bobo caught Kiniski with a kick that split open his nose. Suddenly, Kiniski's headache was unbearable. The crowd was roaring and all of the fans were on Bobo's side. Kiniski frantically kicked, gouged, and used the ropes, but Bobo was too powerful.

"Whatever I did seemed to bounce off his sweating body like tiny peas shot from a pea shooter," Kiniski said. "'What the heck is going on here?' I asked myself. 'I can't even slow this guy down a little bit no matter what I do.'"

Kiniski could barely move. He tried desperately to defend himself. His NWA World heavyweight title was in jeopardy.

Bobo Brazil and Gene Kiniski go after each other during a television interview before a much-anticipated bout in December, 1968.

Kiniski tried to tie up Bobo with arm-locks, but he just didn't have the strength to hold him. Meanwhile, Bobo didn't seem to sense how much trouble his opponent was in. Instead of going for the kill, he respected the skill of the man who had been champion for over two years. Bobo, of course, knew that one mistake could lead to disaster against such a talented champion.

"He thought I was playing possum," Kiniski said. "But I wasn't. He thought I was faking weakness to suck him into a trap."

Nonetheless, Bobo seemed to be on the verge of victory. Kiniski went for an arm-lock, but Bobo broke it with ease. Then Bobo made a crucial mistake—he barely connected with a dropkick. The force of the kick was enough to hurt Kiniski, but Bobo crashed to the mat. Bobo tore ligaments in his side. Now both men were seriously injured. Bobo got up and tried another dropkick. Again, he barely connected and crashed to the mat, this time with his left leg bent underneath his body. Bobo screamed, as if he had broken his leg.

Both men were on the mat, writhing in pain, while the referee started counting. Kiniski barely got up before the ten count. Bobo stayed down. Kiniski was the winner and champion.

Bobo had fallen short of his championship dream. It was the closest he would ever come to winning the NWA World heavyweight title. However, that match had a major impact on history. A few months later, Kiniski lost the title to Dory Funk Jr.

"When you get hit with a head that is as hard as Bobo's, it's the same as if a big guy slugged you over the noggin with a lead pipe," Kiniski said in an interview. "You stay dizzy for hours and you never know what permanent damage has been done to your skull. When I went into the match with Bobo that night, I had a terrible fear of what I knew would surely happen—I was going to be butted."

"The aftereffects of the Bobo Brazil bout did not linger just a day or a week or even a month after I left Los Angeles," Kiniski later revealed. "They are with me to this day. They were with me in Tampa the night I lost my title. They may still be with me for the rest of my life. It is for that reason that I say, Dory, send a letter of thanks to Bobo Brazil. You owe it to him."

Bobo never received a letter from Dory Funk. Never even a thank you. Bobo had changed wrestling history, but had nothing to show for it.

"I was heartbroken," Bobo said. "I had wrestled the best match of my life, but I still wasn't champion. But I vowed to never give up."

7 The War Against the Sheik

In the 1960s, Bobo Brazil fought several violent matches against sadistic opponents like Fred Blassie, one of the cruelest rulebreakers in wrestling history. Blassie never showed mercy to an opponent. One night, Blassie learned that Bobo had referred to him as "an ancient has-been."

"Nobody is going to burn me," Blassie vowed. "When I get him in that ring tonight, I'm going to make him eat his words."

From the beginning of the match, Blassie tore into Bobo. He forced Bobo into the corner and sank his teeth into his neck. Bobo couldn't believe what Blassie had done! Biting was not only against the rules, it was a transgression committed by few rulebreakers. Bobo made a brief comeback, but Blassie was relentless. He hammered him into the ropes with elbow jolts and knee-lifts, then grabbed him around the neck and started choking him to death.

Bobo was in bad shape. He tried to break the choke hold, but couldn't. Blassie's eyes bulged with maniacal delight. The fans pleaded for Bobo to use his Coco Butt, but Bobo couldn't even get his head free. Finally, Bobo summoned his last ounce of

Bobo Brazil takes on The Sheik at the Los Angeles Coliseum in August, 1971.

energy, broke the hold, and Coco-Butted Blassie into bloody submission.

It was a memorable match, as Bobo's NWA world title match against Gene Kiniski in Los Angeles had been. But Bobo's most famous feuds were against his most hated opponent—the United States champion, The Sheik.

In 1969, Bobo battled The Sheik in a spectacular best two-of-three falls match at Olympic Auditorium in Los Angeles. Bobo was waiting in his corner for the time-keeper's bell to ring when The Sheik stormed across the ring and attacked him. The Sheik caught Bobo with a kick in the kidneys, a rabbit punch, a chop to the kidneys, and a stomp. Weakened, Bobo tried to ward off The Sheik, but the crazed wrestler wouldn't relent. The Sheik nearly crippled Bobo with repeated kicks and punches before finishing him off with his "Camel Clutch" for the pin in thirty-one seconds.

When the second fall started, Bobo smartly avoided a charge by The Sheik and then, grabbing The Sheik's ears in both of his hands, nearly ripped them from his head. The Sheik screeched out in pain, tore himself loose from Bobo's fierce grip, and fell to the mat. Bobo came down hard with both knees into The Sheik's back, then knee-lifted the 240-pound wrestler into the air. Bobo applied a reverse headlock for the pin, tying the match at one fall each.

Before the match had started, Abdullah Farouk, The Sheik's manager, had been manacled to the ringpost to keep him from interfering. During the third fall, Farouk handed The Sheik something over the ring apron. The referee and Mr. Moto, Bobo's corner man, grabbed Farouk's hand to see what he was holding. Whatever had been there was gone. Mr. Moto ran into the ring and examined The Sheik. Suddenly, a huge ball of fire flew from The Sheik's hand and into the eyes of Mr. Moto.

Mr. Moto screamed in pain, as if acid were burning his eyes. His horrible screams filled the arena. Bobo ran to Mr. Moto's aid. Mr. Moto was in desperate need for medical attention, so Bobo picked him up and carried him back to the dressing room area, where he could get medical attention. The referee had no choice but to count Bobo out. The American championship still belonged to The Sheik.

"I didn't want to count Bobo out under these conditions," said referee Red Shoes Dugan, "but I had no choice."

"I treasured the championship," said Bobo, "but nothing is so valuable as the health and welfare of a friend. I did what I had to do. Thank God that the damage to Moto's eyes was just superficial. But the doctor said that if he hadn't been able to get immediate treatment, Moto would have been blinded for life."

The feud with The Sheik made Bobo even more popular. Fans loved, and copied, his trademark red and blue silk vests. Meanwhile, Bobo was busy giving as much time as he could to charities. He became a legendary figure in St. Louis, where he teamed with such stars as Dick the Bruiser and Pat O'Connor. He also lost a memorable NWA world title match to Jack Brisco.

However, Bobo's war against The Sheik overshadowed all of his other matches. In 1971, The Sheik had been the United States champion for four years, and Bobo was intent on winning the belt from this despised villain. After all, he was the United States' best hope against this foreign invader.

On May 29, 1971, at Cobo Hall in Detroit, Bobo stepped into the ring for another showdown against The Sheik.

"He was hiding from me, he was running from me, he was avoiding me in every way possible," Bobo told a magazine. "Finally, when it got to the point that he was forced by the commission to put his belt up against me or be stripped of his title, he reluctantly signed for the match."

Bobo wrestled the greatest match of his life and beat The Sheik for the American title.

"I made it to the top only with the help of all of my friends in this area, the people who backed me all the way to the championship," Bobo said. "I will not let these people down. They didn't let me down."

Enraged over his title loss, The Sheik unleashed a brutal assault on Bobo during a rematch. Using a pencil, he gouged Bobo's face and throat. Bobo was sidelined for more than six weeks. The rematch took place on August 27, 1971, outdoors at the Los Angeles Coliseum in front of over 25,000 fans.

> **"Watch out for the pencil, Bobo, watch out for the pencil."**
>
> -Bobo Brazil, to himself against The Sheik

"I remember saying to myself, 'Watch out for the pencil, Bobo, watch out for the pencil,'" Bobo recalled. "When he finally produced it—and I don't know where he hid it since the referee searched him thoroughly before the match began—I was ready for it. I grabbed it away and used it on him."

The crowd went wild. The Sheik, whose forehead was covered in blood, was getting a bit of his own medicine. Then Bobo disposed of the pencil and moved in for a Coco Butt. That's when The Sheik reached into his pants, pulled out a handful of powder, and threw it at Bobo. Bobo turned just in time and only a little of the powder got in his eyes. But that little bit of powder had done its damage. Bobo was temporarily blinded.

"The burning was like nothing I had ever experienced before," Bobo said.

As Bobo writhed on the mat in pain, The Sheik stood over him and sprinkled what was left of the powder onto his body. He also crumpled up the plastic bag that had contained the powder and tossed it onto Bobo. There wasn't anything Bobo could do to stop this humiliation.

"This was 100 times worse than the pencil," Bobo said. "And I'm telling you right now, I swear I'll get The Sheik if it's the last thing I do."

Bobo and The Sheik exchanged the U.S. title three more times over the next three years as they fought across the country. Their epic battles in Detroit never failed to draw sellout crowds. On July 5, 1975, The Sheik beat Bobo in Detroit for

Bobo Brazil and The Sheik had one of the most bitter feuds in the sport.

his eighth U.S. title, tying Bobo's record. A year later, Bobo won the title for the ninth and final time. The feud had taken an exhausting toll on both men.

"I couldn't even begin to tell you how many miles I've traveled in my wrestling career," Bobo said. "But I can tell you that I've traveled many, many millions of miles. Sometimes I think I can tell you the airlines' schedules better than their own travel people. But how else can I be a fighting champion—one who goes out and defends his title against any and every worthy opponent?

"I know a lot of so-called champions pick and choose their spots. Maybe they wrestle twice a week and complain the rest of the time about how tired they are. I'll tell you this—I've worked too hard for this belt and it means too much to me not to defend it as often as I can. Besides, all this regular work keeps me in great physical shape. I can't afford to relax. It's when you relax, you get lazy, or overconfident, that you get beaten. I hope that won't happen to me."

By the mid-1970s, Bobo had been wrestling for over twenty-five years. And he still hadn't slowed down.

8 The Road Not Taken

Two roads diverged in a wood, and I —
I took the one less traveled by,
And that has made all the difference.
**—Robert Frost,
"The Road Not Taken"**

A person never knows what life will bring. In the 1940s, Bobo Brazil could have never guessed that by the 1970s, he would be one of the most famous and most popular wrestlers in the world. But he did know that he had made the right choice by becoming a professional wrestler. Joe Savoldi had been right too. At the peak of his earning power, Bobo was making over $200,000 a year.

Bobo was always willing to take the road less traveled by. One day, he was on his way to a television interview when he happened to pass a Boys Club. He looked in the window and saw a bunch of young boys wrestling on the mats.

"I just had to stop and encourage some of the boys, and well, you know the rest," Bobo explained. "I feel that the youth of America, they need us, and if I can sacrifice a little now and then, by golly, I'm going to do it, no matter what the cost. I believe in giving the kids a break. By the way, that interview turned out just fine. I brought a couple of kids from the Boys Club with me."

In 1977, when Bobo lost the United States title to future wrestling great Ric Flair, the golden age of professional wrestling crossed paths with the new age of professional wrestling. In 1978, a match took place that nobody would have dreamed of—Bobo teamed with The Sheik.

"It was weird," Bobo said. "There were so many nights when we tried to kill each other, and there we were standing on the same side of the ring. I felt like giving him a Coco Butt just for old time's sake, and I betcha he felt like pulling out a pencil and gouging my eyes, just for old time's sake, too."

Bobo finally retired in the mid-1980s and settled down in Benton Harbor, where he ran a bar called Bobo's Grill. Bobo eventually admitted that he wasn't cut out for the restaurant business. He preferred wrestling and working with children. He contributed his time to charities, wrestled occasionally, and raised money for worthy causes by promoting professional wrestling cards.

"I love this business," Bobo said. "I wish I had made more money in it, but I did very well and supported my family."

In 1994, the WWF inducted Bobo into its Hall of Fame. And on January 14,

Bobo Brazil eventually lost his United States title to up-and-comer Ric Flair, now a wrestling legend—ushering in a new era of champions in the late 1970s.

1998, Bobo suffered a stroke. He was taken to Lakeland Medical Hospital in St. Joseph, Michigan. He died on January 20, 1998, at the age of seventy-four.

"New generations of wrestlers and fans will come and go, but many will always be influenced by Bobo," wrote *Pro Wrestling Illustrated* magazine upon giving Bobo its Editors' Award in 1998. "He was able to break the color barrier, win over fans of all backgrounds, and inspire so many young grapplers. With or without a title belt, he was a worthy champion in their eyes."

Bobo was a champion, a pioneer, and a courageous man who made things possible for others. That's Bobo Brazil's legacy—one to be proud of.

Glossary

armlock Move where one wrestler pulls the opponent's arm behind his or her back by placing his or her arm between the opponent's arm and back.

card List of matches on a wrestling show.

clothesline Offensive move in which the attacking wrestler sticks out his or her arm and uses it to strike the opponent in the neck.

The counter attack/counter wrestling

Defensive strategy in which the wrestler's primary goal is to break or wrestle his or her way out of his or her opponent's offensive move.

countout When a wrestler is counted out for leaving the ring for twenty seconds or more. The referee begins his or her count at one the moment the wrestler leaves the ring. A wrestler who is counted out is disqualified.

curfew Prescribed time at which a wrestling card must end. Certain states, such as New York, have had eleven o'clock curfews for wrestling cards.

feud   Series of matches between two wrestlers or two tag teams. Many times one wrestler will bad-mouth or sneak attack the other wrestler.

flying head scissors   Aerial move in which a wrestler leaps into the air, wraps his or her legs around the opponent's neck, and tugs him or her to the mat.

foreign object   Illegal object used in the ring, such as a chair or a pencil.

gimmick   Personality of a wrestler.

manager   Person responsible for over-seeing a wrestler's inside-the-ring and outside-the-ring activities. Managers often take care of a wrestler's business affairs (such as signing contracts and arranging matches) and also assist with strategy.

pin When either both shoulders or both shoulder blades are held in contact with the mat for three continuous seconds. A pin ends a match.

pinfall Win achieved by a pin.

promoter Person responsible for hiring and contracting the wrestlers for a card or federation. The promoter is also responsible for deciding the match-ups for a card.

scientific match   Match between two
  or more wrestlers, in which the com-
  batants rely mostly on amateur
  wrestling moves, rather than kicking
  and punching.

small package   Counter-wrestling
  move in which the wrestler being
  pinned grabs the opponent's legs or
  upper body, rolls him or her over, and
  places him or her into pinning position.

submission hold   Move that
  makes an opponent give up without
  being pinned.

For More Information

Magazines

Pro Wrestling Illustrated, The Wrestler, Inside Wrestling, Wrestle America, and *Wrestling Superstars*
London Publishing Co.
7002 West Butler Pike
Ambler, PA 19002
(215) 643-6385

WCW Magazine
P.O. Box 420235
Palm Coast, FL 32142-0235

(800) WCW-MAGS (929-6247)

Web site: http://www.wcw.com

WOW Magazine

McMillen Communications

P.O. Box 500

Missouri City, TX 77459-9904

(800) 310-7047

e-mail:

 woworder@mcmillencomm.com

Web site:

http://www.wowmagazine.com

Web Sites

Dory Funk's Web Site

Web site: http: //www.dory-funk.com

Professional Wrestling Online Museum
Web site:
http://www.wrestlingmuseum.com

Pro Wrestling Torch
Web site: http://www.pwtorch.com

World Championship Wrestling
Web site: http://www.wcw.com

World Wrestling Federation
Web site: http://www.wwf.com

For Further Reading

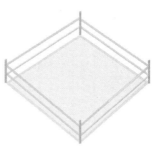

Albano, Lou, Bert Randolph Sugar, and
　　Michael Benson. *The Complete Idiot's
　　Guide to Pro Wrestling,* 2nd ed. New
　　York: Alpha Books, 2000.

Archer, Jeff. *Theater in a Squared
　　Circle.* New York: White-Boucke
　　Publishing, 1998.

Cohen, Dan. *Wrestling Renegades:
　　An In-Depth Look at Today's
　　Superstars of Pro Wrestling.* New
　　York: Archway, 1999.

Conner, Floyd. *Wrestling's Most Wanted: The Top 10 Book of Pro Wrestling's Outrageous Performers, Punishing Piledrivers, and Other Oddities*. Washington, DC: Brasseys, 2001.

Farley, Cal, and E.L. Howe. *Two Thousand Sons: The Story of Cal Farley's Boys Ranch*. Canaan, NH: Phoenix Publishing, 1987.

Greenberg, Keith Elliot. *Pro Wrestling: From Carnivals to Cable TV*. Minneapolis, MN: Lerner, 2000.

Hofstede, David. *Slammin': Wrestling's Greatest Heroes and Villains*. New York: ECW Press, 1999.

Kowalski, Walter. *Killer Pics: A Collection of Images from a Pro-Wrestling Legend*. Lafayette, CO: White-Boucke, 2000.

LeBell, "Judo" Gene. *Pro-Wrestling Finishing Holds*. Los Angeles, CA: Pro-Action, 1985.

Mazer, Sharon. *Professional Wrestling: Sport and Spectacle*. Jackson, MS: University Press of Mississippi, 1998.

Myers, Robert. *The Professional Wrestling Trivia Book*. Boston: Branden Books, 1999.

Works Cited

Berger, Ira, and Sheldon Widelitz. "Golden
    Grappler." *Italian American Magazine*
    March, 1977, pp. 45–49.

"Bruno Sammartino Beat 21 Opponents All
    In One Night." *The Wrestler*, May, 1972,
    pp. 32–37.

Jerome, James F. "Wrestling Champ
    Sammartino, A Big Man At The Bank."
    People, July 1, 1974, pp. 19–21.

Kupferberg, Herbert. "The Rough (and Rich)
    Life of a Wrestling Champ." *Parade*,
    February 15, 1976, pp. 12–16.

Sammartino, Bruno. *Bruno
    Sammartino: An Autobiography of*

Wrestling's Living Legend. Pittsburgh: Imagine, 1990.

Bruno Sammartino. "My Three Toughest Opponents." *Wrestling World,* June, 1968, pp. 55–63.

"Sammartino Speaks Out." *Wrestling World,* October, 1967, pp. 19–23.

Verigan, Bill. "Pedro, Bruno in Curfew Draw and All's Well." *Daily News,* October 2, 1972, p. 78.

Index

Photo Credits

All photos courtesy of *Pro Wrestling Illustrated* except pp. 7, 18-19 © AP/Worldwide.

Series Design and Layout

Geri Giordano